Traders Troubleshooting Tools

A Collection of Aphorisms, Quotes and Trading Tips by

Bill M. Williams, PhD
Founder of the
Profitunity Trading Group

Annotated and Edited by
Justine Williams-Lara
and Marcus D. Lara

Traders Troubleshooting Tools

Copyright © 2012

Library of Congress Control #
2011905232

ISBN: 978-0-9835106-1-1

Published in the
United States of America

August 23, 2012

About This Book

Traders Troubleshooting Tools was created to provide a summary of Bill Williams' many trading aphorisms, quotes, and trading tips. We call them "tools" because these simple ideas enable minor adjustments to our thinking, which traders often require. As experienced traders know, it is imperative to remain centered in the present during the trading day.

The vast majority of the aphorisms and phrases in this book have been used in one of our three books, home study courses, and tutorials.

The rest are from Bill's journals and unpublished writings on the number one obstacle for traders around the world: our own thoughts!

Take your time to read and digest these thoughts and ideas. You will be reminded of the natural simplicity of the mechanics of the markets. Then, when you are operating with the proper mindset in the markets, you will not only improve your relationship with the markets, but also with your business associates, your friends and family, and bring more peace and prosperity to your trading life.

Dedicated to a Master Trader

This book is a tribute to Bill M. Williams who decided to give the vast knowledge he acquired back to provide trading education, and to his wife, Ellen Williams for supporting him in his enduring efforts to share his methodology with traders from around the world.

In his 81st year of life, he still trades the markets every day.

Additional Reading by

Bill M. Williams, PhD, and Justine Williams-Lara

"Trading Chaos: 2nd Edition"
Wiley Publishing 2004

"New Trading Dimensions"
Wiley Publishing 1998

"Trading Chaos"
Wiley Publishing 1995

For more information about
Profitunity Trading Group
visit http://Profitunity.com

Take a deep breath.

Take a deep breath, release the stress of the past, and be fully present in the current moment.

You have everything you need.

You have everything you need to be a successful trader. Every decision you made and the actions you have taken, brought you here to learn what you need to learn to realize your dream.

Simplify your trading.

When we find ourselves struggling in our trading, we do not need a new indicator or a new strategy. We need a new outlook.

Trading is not a race.

There are unlimited opportunities for profit in the markets. Let go of the feeling of being in a hurry and the market will provide the opportunity.

Focus on the positive.

If we can focus on the positive in every trade, then we are able to keep an open mind and learn from the market.

*All life and trading
is a dream.*

We say this not because it isn't real, but because we all see the world through our own filters that skew our perspective. This gives us our own outlook on reality and the unique experience we create for ourselves along the way.

Know when to say
yes or no.

Just as you learn the rules of driving a vehicle on the road, you can learn to effectively navigate the markets by only following the signals on a chart.

There are no bad markets.

The markets are neutral so they cannot be bad or good. The markets are either tradable or not tradable based on market conditions, our own account value, risk tolerance, and individual trading style.

Cooperate with the market.

When we cooperate with the market
we allow it to show us where it is
going. Realize that when you are in
disagreement with the market, then
you are in disagreement with reality.

*Understand the market,
understand yourself.*

By finding the markets that best suit
our personality, we can then utilize our
trading skills to their highest efficacy
and bring more peace to our trading
experience.

Be open with the market.

When we are open to the market, we are open to the abundance of the physical world. The market can provide all that we need to earn a living, but we still must do our part and be fully present while we are trading.

The market is your teacher.

Every day is an opportunity to learn from the market. It is necessary to keep an open mind, as every trade will teach you something about your operating system if you pay attention to the lesson being offered.

*No one really trades
the markets.*

We all trade our belief systems. When
we place our trades, we bring these
beliefs with us into the markets. The
opportunity for profit exists because
we all have different beliefs about
what is happening in the world.

I am a good trader.

You only need one affirmation and this is it. Read these words every day until you don't have to read them anymore.

Want what the market wants.

When we want what the market wants, we allow it to be exactly where it is now. This idea is the Holy Grail of trading and is the vehicle to get us to the place of oneness with the market that we are all seeking to experience.

We are the market.

When we are viewing our charts we are looking at a composite view of humanity. Over time we are able to connect all the dots to realize that there is no market without all of the individual traders who make it up.

*The market is
what you think it is.*

To some traders, the market is a dangerous and threatening place, full of unseen traps. To others, the market is a bountiful garden where you reap the rewards of your decisions to play it cool and go with the flow.

*Successful trading comes
by letting go.*

In any endeavor, holding onto the outcome creates an energy blockage. When we are on the edge of a cliff, the best thing to do is enjoy the view. When we are trading on the edge, we must trust our indicators and let go.

There is no such thing as overbought or oversold.

The market's purpose is to find the balance between buyers and sellers, which is expressed by a change in price. Thus, the markets cannot be overbought or oversold. It is best to abolish these words from your vocabulary and forget them.

*Great traders are
good observers.*

Essential to becoming a great trader
is to first be a good observer. Over
time we learn to make quick decisions
from our observations and effectively
implement our strategies. This is the
path to mastering the markets.

*Chaos is a higher
form of order.*

Chaos is another word for the energy of new incoming information on its way to be assimilated into what already exists. This new incoming information is what creates price movement in the markets.

You are the executive decision maker.

As an individual trader, you are the CEO of your own corporation. With every trade you have no one to praise if you win or anyone to blame if you lose. It is all up to you.

Should have, could have, would have.

We can spend our lives looking at missed trades. Rather than negate our experiences we need to recognize these trade set-ups as learning tools and utilize them in our trading journey as we move forward.

You can't be grateful and angry at the same time.

When we are living in gratitude, anger cannot penetrate our being. Every day we have the choice to be grateful for what is, or to be resentful about what is not.

What animal does the market represent?

Is the market a shark, a coyote, a cunning viper, or is it a playful puppy on its way to becoming your best friend? You decide what animal the market resembles to you and you give it power over you with the energy you feed it.

Trading is an art form.

Consider yourself as an artist as traders who read charts for technical analysis are now called "chartists." Trading off of charts is a learned visual art of interpreting the charts, combined with specialized training in methods known to provide profits.

The market does two things.

All that is really going on is that some traders believe that the market is going up while other traders believe that the market is going down. And so it does.

*Value comes from
our perception.*

We create value based on our perception and project an object's worth through the story we place on that object. This is also true in all trading.

*Trading education
is the key.*

Trading education is the best solution to preserving capital, as when we are trading in the live markets, our money can easily move into the accounts of those who are educated and experienced.

The market is never wrong.

The market is where it is because that's where it's supposed to be. When we change our mind about the market being wrong, the market will change and all will be right again.

It's all speculation.

Speculators get paid for buying what nobody wants when nobody wants it and selling what everybody wants when everybody wants it.

Don't say another negative thing.

Take a few minutes to reflect on all the obstacles you have overcome to be where you are now. From this perspective there is no room to complain about your trading experiences.

Healthy choices lead to healthy trading.

A healthy trader has a strong mind, and lives a well-balanced lifestyle. It is very easy to get out of balance so we must strive to eliminate any unnecessary stress caused by poor choices.

We learn from every trade.

Just as there is a lesson to learn from every trade, every moment is an opportunity to learn and grow. In trading what we end up learning is mostly about is our self and human nature.

Trading is an energy exchange.

All life is an energy exchange. But in trading, we do not get more by doing more. We get more by doing less.

We were born to trade.

Humans have been trading since the beginning of time. Not only do we trade for goods and services, we also trade our time every day. When we exchange our time for currency or work for a paycheck, we are trading.

Donate a percentage of your profits.

Making regular donations to charity is a common trait of many successful traders. Of all the traders we have trained, those who give regularly also tend to be happier and healthier people.

*Reality is created
in real time.*

Modern science supports the idea that an individual's notion of reality in the world is being created by their own mind at each and every moment, just like the price on a real time chart.

*Good traders make
good choices.*

It is imperative that a trader understands the importance of making good choices in all areas of life as one good decision leads to another.

The reason we are here is to find out who we are.

We are all on the path of discovering ourselves. As traders, not only do we get to see what we are made of, but we also get to pay for our own self-examination.

The harder you push against the flow, the harder it pushes back.

We make most of our trading mistakes when we try to force a trade. This is because the market will always generate an opposing force to counter the energy imbalance and restore harmony through humility.

*Trading is an expedition
in personal growth.*

In trading we can simultaneously conquer our fears and realize our dreams. So every time we make a trade, we need to take a look at ourselves to see if we are heading in the right direction.

Trust your first instinct.

When we trust our intuition and follow our set of trading rules, we usually find that we make our best trades.

Master your mind.
Master the market.

Before you can master the market, you must first master your mind. Do not allow the market to be your master. It follows that once you have mastered your mind it is easier to become a master of all things.

Profits follow the
path of least resistance.

Money is currency, which is a form of
energy. Energy will always follow the
path of least resistance determined
by the always underlying and usually
unseen structure.

Have faith in your system.

The most successful traders are those who have a great sense of faith in their education, their trading system, and their own ability to make good choices.

The outer world is a reflection of the inner world.

In order to find peace in the outer world, we first must find peace within ourselves. As we become more conscious of our power to create peace, the rest of the world will respond and also become more conscious.

Do not seek the opinions of others.

It is better to be your own analyst. Rather than allowing outside opinions to affect our trading, it is best to avoid them and not follow anyone else's recommendations.

*Trading is all in
the approach.*

Life and trading is about how we
approach it. How we approach the
markets usually determines what we
take away from the markets after
they close.

Flexible traders never get bent out of shape.

By being less rigid in our trading, we are able to go with the flow. Rather than pushing the river, we become the river and find the natural flow of the market.

The market is not your problem.

The problem is that you think the market is your problem. For most traders, learning to keep profits is necessary in order to find a solution.

There is no such thing as bullish or bearish consensus.

When taking a consensus only a small percentage of traders are being interviewed. Since they represent only a fraction of shares or contracts being traded at any given time, there is no way to get a true summary of opinions.

*Most traders lose
because they are lost.*

They are either using the wrong maps,
using the wrong trading paradigm, or
stuck in the wrong thinking.

The market has one job.

It finds the exact point where there is an equal disagreement on value and an agreement on price.

You don't need to transform your trading.

You need to transcend it. We cannot out-think our problems. We have to outgrow them.

*Price is an effect
and not a cause.*

The current price is the single most accurate representation of reality, and the only absolute truth in the market.

*Trading is the most
naked therapy in the world.*

We all have issues with money. Trading brings these issues to the surface where we are able to create more understanding of how money and our decisions affect all areas of our life.

*Emotional management is
the most difficult barrier
to profitable trading.*

If we can get our emotions out of the
way and overlook the interference,
we can follow the signals and become
more profitable traders.

Most traders win or lose to the same degree that they understand themselves.

Because the markets are a reflection of human behavior, traders who are in tune with their inner trader are on the path to become better traders.

*The primary function of
the market is communication.*

The market shares the information
it receives by generating a real-time
composition of the beliefs of all the
traders in the market.

*Trend trading is
like flying a kite.*

When you catch the trend your trade
will fly on its own after it gets off the
ground.

Consistent winners have mastered the art of dancing with the market.

Remember that in order to dance well and find joy in dancing, we must allow ourselves to be moved by the music and go with the tune rather than follow a rigid agenda.

Don't trade
your last mistake.

Traders generally trade off of their last mistake rather than being fully present in the current market. If we want to trade at our best we must face the reality of today's market.

*There is no such
thing as a bad trader.*

There is only a trader who has been well trained or poorly trained.

Trading is a game of fantasy.

In this game we make what isn't, more important than what is. The reason we play this game is because we have the fantasy that our future reality will somehow be better than our present reality.

Risk is a turn-on in life.

Risk is addictive. When taking financial risks, chemicals are created in our brain and we get addicted to taking more risks, just as if risk were a drug.

Your beliefs about the market create your reality of the market.

We project all of our thoughts, desires, and beliefs about the market into our trades, and it reflects them back to the same degree of our self-understanding.

*Most money management
plans don't work.*

If you place your protection based on
a percentage loss you are not trading
the market, you are trading your
wallet or your bank account, which has
absolutely no relation to the markets
or what is happening in the markets.

Money is not your motivation.

You think you are seeking to profit, but what you are really seeking is permanence and peace of mind.

The market is a creature of chaos.

Without chaos there would be no change in price. The market would not exist without uncertainty caused by new incoming information from events happening around the world.

Ideas rule the market.

We create our trading opportunities based on our ideas about what is happening in our reality, or what we think is going to happen in the very near future.

Trading is an inside job.

The inside job in trading is the growth of the inner being. It follows that if you want to be a successful trader you must be willing to do the inner work.

*Let go and grow
in the market.*

Let go and give the market room to breathe. The market is going to do what it is going to do regardless of what you do.

*To be a winning trader
you must be ok with losing.*

If you can't afford to lose, you can't afford to win. You are going to have losing days just as you are going to have winning days.

In the markets, every day is a new day.

The market does not remember who you are from the previous day, previous month, or previous year. Every day the market gives you the freedom to begin again.

The ego is our biggest enemy in the market.

Losing does not mean you are wrong and winning does not mean you are right. There will be losing trades and there will be winning trades. Both are equally important to all traders.

The markets are an
ever-changing social process.

Because all markets are related, their movements impact each other, making them all socially interdependent, even more than in our human relationships.

No one can control the market.

There is no one out to get you in the market, and no one can control the market. Be careful anyway.

How we respond to our thoughts is more important than the thoughts themselves.

You can respond with crazy, catatonic, or conscious. At every moment we have the choice of living with resistance or with a welcoming spirit and an open mind.

Creating resonance between your intellect and your intuition is the key to making consistent profits.

Harmony between your thoughts and actions creates a solid trading foundation and a strong platform to build upon.

We don't need more experience, we need more in-sperience.

In a society that is over-stimulated, the illusion exists that everything is outside of ourselves. However, the opposite is true. Reality exists inside of each and every one of us.

Move from thinking about the market to thinking with the market.

All that we need from the market is to provide us with signals so we can take the appropriate action. We do not need to be consumed with it in order to be in tune with it.

Walk away from trading the how to trading the now.

A proficient trader no longer thinks of the process of trading or questions their methodology. They simply place trades based on the indicators displayed on their charts.

To change our trading course we must change our underlying structure.

Trying to change your trading without first changing your mental state is like trying to convince yourself that a merry-go-round has a destination.

If you are expecting perfection, you are setting yourself up for disappointment.

Having the correct personal attitude in all your trades is more important that being correct in every trade.

Don't let the data dictate your day.

Information changes every moment so do not live by the mistaken notion that who you are is somehow affected by what happens in the markets.

Stick with your strategy.

If you are going to implement a trading strategy based on a specific set of rules, then you should follow through with it.

Quiet your trader mind.

The vast majority of thinking is detrimental to personal peace and profits in the market. The goal here is to unthink.

Trading is a tool for enlightenment.

Trading requires dedication and discipline and is not an activity for victims or poor-me personalities.

Trading can provide a path to your higher self if you are willing to pay attention, listen, and learn.

About Bill M. Williams, PhD, and Profitunity Trading Group

As the founder of the Profitunity Trading Group, Bill M. Williams created not only a holistic approach to trading the markets but also a trading philosophy that is now embraced on every continent around the world. Bill first began trading in 1959 and started educating traders in 1984 sharing his strategies and trading methodology in seminars in Chicago's thriving financial district.

When he first began teaching there was no charting software and his talks on psychology were sometimes perceived as being ridiculous and nonsensical.

But as the fields of technical analysis and trading psychology grew together, so did his reputation as one of the top trading teachers in the world along with other legends of trading such as Larry Williams and Jake Bernstein.

After growing up poor during the depression on a farm in Alabama he served as a pilot in the U.S. Air Force. Then he attended Auburn University where he earned a degree in engineering physics followed by a PhD in clinical psychology.

His education also includes a lifetime of holistic studies of the mind and body including the healing arts, bodywork, mathematics, physics, metaphysics,

quantum physics, as well as music, nutrition, gardening and horticulture.

He authored three international best-selling trading books that have been published into over seven languages; Trading Chaos, New Trading Dimensions, and Trading Chaos: 2nd Edition.

He created many well-known trading indicators including but not limited to the Profitunity Alligator, the Super AO (Awesome Oscillator), the MFI, the Blue Light Special, the Breakout Fractal, and the Squat Bar; all components of the Profitunity Wiseman Indicators. He also developed his own methods for trading fractals of the Elliott Wave.

Besides the three trading books and the assortment of indicators, his wife and business partner Ellen Williams created and recorded the Profitunity Autogenic Training System, an anti-stress and relaxation audio program that has been a major component and required exercise for students in each of the previous and present versions of the Profitunity Home Study Course.

Bill's trading methodology continues to be taught by the co-authors of this book, his daughter Justine Williams-Lara and her husband Marcus D. Lara, in their offices in Southern California and at tutorial training events and conferences held in cities such as Las Vegas, Chicago, Miami, and Amsterdam.

Together they share in Profitunity's daily operations and provide guidance and support to students of the Profitunity Trading Group worldwide.

With students in over 60 countries around the world we are dedicated to providing support to all of our clients, no matter what level of trading experience they have. We strive to assist all of our students to uncover their own unique trading style and discover the markets they trade best given their account value and risk tolerance.

Thank you for your support!

Your purchase of this book will support our enduring goal to provide quality educational materials to traders just like you who come from every country in the world.

Good Trading!

Justine & Marcus

Remember these five words...

Want
What
the
Market
Wants

- Bill M. Williams, PhD

For more information about
Profitunity Trading Group
visit:

http://Profitunity.com

CPSIA information can be obtained at www.ICGtesting.com
Printed in the USA
LVOW04s2352010915

452390LV00030B/778/P